D1329358

OCT 01 1973

The Ecumenical Movement

THREE LECTURES

GIVEN AT

THE UNIVERSITY OF THE SOUTH
SEWANEE, TENNESSEE
in March, 1950

BY

THE REV. LEONARD HODGSON, D.D.
Regius Professor of Divinity in the
University of Oxford

I.   1910—1937
II. 1937—1948
III. 1948—1950

THE UNIVERSITY PRESS
THE UNIVERSITY OF THE SOUTH
SEWANEE, TENNESSEE
1 9 5 1

BX
9
.H6E
1951

FOREWORD

THROUGH the courtesy of my one time pupil, the Rev. Dr. Richard H. Wilmer, Jr., now Chaplain at Sewanee, I was invited there to give three lectures on the Ecumenical Movement during a visit to America now just ended. One or two of those who heard them expressed the desire to see them in print.

In so far as they have any right to have been given before a university audience, it must be as a contribution to the study of recent ecclesiastical history. The history is so recent, and I have myself been so intimately connected with some of it, that my authority for many of my statements is my own memory. Any judgments expressed are the utterance of my own private opinion; they must not be taken as representing an official view either of the Church of England or of the Faith and Order Movement. Both for mistakes in matters of fact, and for errors in judgment, I am alone responsible.

I want to put on record my great gratitude to Dr. Wilmer and all those many colleagues of his who not only did me the honour of inviting me to lecture, but also made my visit to Sewanee so very enjoyable.

L. H.

R.M.S. Queen Elizabeth,
    May 4th, 1950.

THE ECUMENICAL MOVEMENT

LECTURE I: 1910—1937

(i)

FOR the meaning of the word "ecumenical" we need not go beyond the point when the Greek word *oikoumene* had come to mean the inhabited world. It had come to mean this in the first centuries of our era, and when, in the year 451, the bishops of the Christian Church met in council at Chalcedon they opened their Report with the words "The holy great ecumenical synod", meaning by ecumenical world-wide.

The modern use of the word in the phrase "the ecumenical movement" came about, I believe, as follows. One of the organisations we shall shortly be considering was named in English "The Universal Christian Council for Life and Work". This was translated into French as *Conseil Oecuménique du Christianisme Pratique* and into German as *Oekumenischer Rat für Praktisches Christentum*. From these translations the word spread into common use in English as well as in French and German. Its use by the early Church had given it an ecclesiastical flavour, and it has come to stay as a convenient term to mean "international in the sphere of church relations".

Its use has been criticised on the ground that it does not mean precisely what ecumenical meant as applied to the councils of the early Church. The Amsterdam Assembly of the World Council of Churches is not a modern parallel to the fifth century Council of Chalcedon. This is true. But words change their meanings in the history of linguistic usage, and it is foolish pedantry to refuse to recognise the fact. Who but a pedant would refuse to use the word 'science' to mean anything except the *scientia* of mediaeval Latin? There is no other single word so convenient to mean "international in the sphere of Church relations", and why should we deny ourselves the benefit of this convenience?

Its use has been criticised in particular on the ground that the so-called Ecumenical Movement is not truly ecumenical since it does not include the largest single body of Christians in the modern world, the Roman Catholic Church. It is important to understand the reason for this. The Roman Church cannot join the Movement because it is one of its fundamental principles that it alone is the true Church of Christ: it cannot therefore enter into any organisation in which membership would imply that it is one among others. We understand this position, and can respect it without agreeing with it. But it must be insisted that the Church of Rome does not stand outside the Ecumenical Movement because of any exclusiveness on the Movement's side, any limitation of its would-be truly ecumenical scope. The door is open, and when in God's good time the Roman Church shall come to see the error of its ways and be able to come in, the Movement will become in fact what already it is in intention and in principle. Meanwhile, as expressing that intention and attempting to embody that principle, it can justly think of itself, and call itself, the Ecumenical Movement.

(ii)

The background of the Ecumenical Movement is our divided Christendom. For the first thousand or so years of its life there was, in the main, a single Christian Church. The Christian traveller, arriving in a strange town on a Saturday, did not have to go hunting around to find the church of his own denomination in which to worship next day. This is not the place to discuss the causes of the divisions which put an end to that happy state of affairs. I think myself that it is a mistake to

regard them as wholly due to doctrinal or ecclesiastical disagreements among Christians.   However that may be, what we
have to deal with to-day is the result of the eleventh-century
division between the Churches of East and West, and the further break up of the Western Church in the sixteenth century.

Ignoring for the sake of convenience certain minor differences, Christendom to-day may be thought of as consisting of
seven great families: Eastern Orthodox, Roman Catholic, Anglican, Lutheran, Calvinist, Independent, and Methodist.[1] I use
the word 'families' because that seems to me best to convey the
kind of relationship in which a member of any one of them
feels himself to stand towards his fellow members. Our Christian traveller, be he Anglican, Lutheran, Baptist or what not,
feels himself to be at home among brothers and sisters wher-
ever in the world he finds himself among others of the same
denomination.

Each of these seven families has by now spread all over the
world, and each, looking back over some centuries[2] of growth
and development, sees itself to have been both blessed and used
by God. We may differ in the extent to which we hold that
some particular element in doctrine, discipline or church
order must in theory be essential to the unity of the church;
we cannot deny the empirical fact that in each of these families,
Congregationalist as much as Orthodox or Anglican, we have a
world-wide body whose members are conscious of belonging
together in a community that can look back on manifest evidence
of divine favour.

After the disruptions of the sixteenth century the newly divided Churches were fully occupied in pursuing their own lines

---

[1]In this rough but convenient classification Calvinist includes Churches officially
described as Reformed or Presbyterian; Independent includes those which stress the
autonomy of the local congregation or of the individual Christian, e.g. Congrega-
tional and Baptist Churches and the Society of Friends.

[2]Of the Methodist family it may be said that in a short time it has fulfilled a
long time.

of development. They had not much time for being interested
in one another, except in so far as each was concerned to show
that the others were wrong and it was right. But towards the
end of the last century there came signs of a movement of the
Spirit of God turning men's minds to a new kind of interest,
moving Christians in one family to think of those in others as
allies in a common cause rather than as rivals and competitors.
It began with different groups being moved independently to
embark on different lines of activity: some saw one thing need-
ing to be done, some another. It took time for them to realise
that the different organisations which came into being were
different expressions of one movement of the Spirit. The history of the Ecumenical Movement in the period covered by
these lectures covers the rise of these independent movements,
the discovery of their inter-relatedness, and re-organisation in
the light of this discovery.

The various independent movements with which it all began
may for convenience be classified under three heads.

A. Movements aiming at the co-ordination of existing church
work, so as to promote co-operation and avoid undesirable over-
lapping and rivalry. E.g. The World Student Christian Federation, and the International Missionary Council.

B. Movements aiming at bringing the Christian conscience
to bear on the practical problems of the contemporary world.
E.g. The World Alliance for International Friendship through
the Churches, and the Universal Christian Council for Life and
Work.

C. Movements aiming directly at the discussion of the doctrinal disagreements underlying the disunion of Christendom.
E.g. The World Conference on Faith and Order.

The distinction between B. and C. may be illustrated as follows. In B. the churches may be pictured as represented by
a number of men standing shoulder to shoulder in a circle, fac-

ing outwards, looking on the world and its problems, and asking, "How can we unitedly bring the Christian conscience to bear?" Then for C. we see each man in the picture turning about on the spot on which he stands, so that they now face one another across the circle and ask, "Why must we face the world separately, taking such care not to tread on one another's toes? Why cannot we all be in full union and communion and speak to the world as one Church?"

In my next lecture I shall be speaking of how these independent movements discovered themselves to be parallel expressions of one underlying movement of the Spirit, and of how the steps taken to give effect to this discovery led to the formation of the World Council of Churches and the recognition of it as the focal point of the Ecumenical Movement as a whole. In preparation for that we must now devote the rest of this lecture to the history of some of the independent movements during the period of their independence.

(iii)

A. *The World Student Christian Federation and the International Missionary Council*

The oldest of the movements I have mentioned is the World Student Christian Federation. It was organised in 1895. I can myself remember in my undergraduate days at Oxford hearing Dr. John R. Mott address a W.S.C.F. meeting in 1909. That was the year before the Edinburgh Missionary Conference of 1910, the event with which the history of the Ecumenical Movement may, for practical purposes, be said to begin. Behind that Conference lay the experience of international and interdenominational work gained by Dr. Mott and others in the W.S.C.F. That is what made it possible in a Christendom as yet nervous of any such inter-church activities.

It is difficult for us to-day to realise how novel, how bold, and how difficult it was, forty years ago, to plan a conference of representatives of divided churches. It was only made possible by its organisers giving a definite undertaking that its discussions should be confined to practical issues in missionary policy and method, and that no questions concerning either faith or church order should be raised. The giving of this guarantee was necessary to allay suspicions and to secure a genuinely interdenominational conference. Preliminary studies by eight commissions prepared the material for its consideration. It met, and its meeting, if not the actual beginning of the Ecumenical Movement, was the source of much that determined the course of its later development.

The churches had agreed to take part in a missionary conference, but it was eleven years before it issued in any permanent standing organisation. Doubtless the delay was partly due to the 1914-1918 war, but the following account of the formation of the International Missionary Council shows that it took time for the advocates of co-operation to overcome the traditional hesitancy of many of their fellow churchmen.

'In June, 1920, the first international post-war missionary conference was held at the château of Crans, on the shores of Lake Geneva. At this conference there were delegates from Missionary organizations in North America, South America, France, Great Britain, Holland, Norway, Sweden, Denmark, Finland, and Germany. Here the formation of an International Missionary Conference was proposed. This proposal was later approved by the Churches interested, and the first International Missionary Council met at Lake Mohonk, N. Y., in October, 1921. There the Council completed its organization, and elected officers as follows: Chairman, John R. Mott; Secretaries, J. H. Oldham, A. L. Warnshuis; Treasurer, James M. Speers. No German leaders were present at this Conference. India, China, and Japan were represented. The Council met again at Oxford in July 1923. To this Conference the German Missions sent official representatives. Here, after much discussion and prayer, an agreement was arrived at as to the possibility of missionary co-operation in the face of doctrinal difference. That agreement was as follows:

"The International Missionary Council has never sought, nor is it its function, to work out a body of doctrinal opinions of its own. The only doctrinal opinions in the Council are those which the various members bring with them into it from the Churches and missionary boards to which they belong. It is no part of the duty of the Council to discuss the merits of those opinions, still less to determine doctrinal questions. But it has never been found in practice that in consequence of this the Council is left with nothing but an uncertain mass of conflicting opinions. . . . When we have been gathered together we have experienced a growing unity among ourselves in which we recognize the influence of the Holy Spirit. . . . Every piece of co-operation in work which this Council or any Council connected with it encourages or guides, is confined to those Churches or missions which freely and willingly take part in it. It would be entirely out of harmony with the spirit of our movement to press for such co-operation in work as would be felt to compromise doctrinal principles or strain consciences." "[3]

From that time till now the International Missionary Council has played an increasingly important part in the life of the Churches. It has assembled further world missionary conferences at Jerusalem in 1928, and at Tambaram, India, in 1938. At Tambaram it became clear that Christendom should no longer be thought of as consisting of Churches in Christian countries and mission fields in heathen lands, but of Churches in different parts of the world which were simply to be dis-

---

[3] G. J. Slosser: *Christian Unity, its History and Challenge* (New York, 1929) pp. 256-7.

inguished as Older and Younger. That change of terminology, with the change of mental outlook which it involves, has become characteristic of present day missionary thought and speech. It has come about as a result of the Tambaram Conference of the I.M.C.

The second world war, and other circumstances, have prevented the holding of any further such large missionary conferences. But an enlarged meeting of the Executive Committee of the I.M.C. was held at Whitby, near Toronto, Canada, in 1948, and an Eastern Asia Conference at Bangkok, Siam, in December, 1949.

World Youth Conferences, organised by the W.S.C.F., have been held at Amsterdam in 1938 and Oslo in 1947. It was as General Secretary of the W.S.C.F. that Dr. W. A. Visser 't Hooft gained the ecumenical experience, and manifested the ability, that led to his being chosen in 1939 to be the first General Secretary of the World Council of Churches.

B. *The Universal Christian Council for Life and Work.*

For the origin of this movement we look back to the time of the first world war. In 1914 concern that the Churches internationally ought to do something to prevent war had produced The World Alliance for International Friendship through the Churches. By 1916 some of its members had come to feel that there was a wider range of problems in the contemporary world with which the Christian conscience should be concerned. This was voiced in that year at a meeting of the Federal Council of Churches in America. The idea of an international conference on this wider front was taken up and pushed forward by Archbishop Söderblom of Uppsala, Sweden. A preparatory conference was held at Geneva, Switzerland, in 1920. The first full scale world conference on Life and Work met at Stockholm in 1925.

It was intended that this conference, like the Edinburgh missionary conference of 1910, should eschew questions of faith and order. Some of its sponsors were influenced by the notion that while the discussion of doctrinal differences would only result in setting churches further apart, there would be general agreement about the demands of the Christian conscience: the practical questions about how to make those demands effective could be separated from doctrinal questions and made a profitable subject for co-operative discussion. The official statement of the aim of the conference was as follows:

"The Conference on Life and Work, without entering into questions of Faith and Order, aims to unite the different Churches in common practical work, to furnish the Christian conscience with an organ of expression in the midst of the great spiritual movement of our time, and to insist that the principles of the Gospel be applied to the solution of the contemporary social and international problems".[4]

With this aim in view, the Conference took for its programme the following five subjects:

(i) The Purpose of God for Humanity and the Duty of the Church.
(ii) The Church and Economic and Industrial Problems.
(iii) The Church and International Relations.
(iv) The Church and Christian Education.
(v) Methods of Co-operative and Federative Efforts by the Christian Communions.

There were present some five hundred representatives of the Churches of twenty-seven nations. The four presidents of the Conference were officially Archbishop Söderblom of Sweden, the Archbishop of Canterbury, the Oecumenical Patriarch of

[4]Quoted from Slosser, op. cit., p. 294.

Constantinople, and Dr. Arthur J. Brown of the Presbyterian Church in the U.S.A. Of these, Archbishop Söderblom and Dr. Brown were present in person; the Archbishop of Canterbury was represented by Bishop Theodore Woods of Winchester, and the Oecumenical Patriarch by his Exarch in Western Europe, Archbishop Germanos.

A Continuation Committee was appointed to continue the work after the adjournment of the Conference. Bishop Theodore Woods was its first chairman; after his death in 1932 he was succeeded by the present Bishop of Chichester, Dr. G. K. A. Bell. A permanent office was established in Geneva with Dr. Hans Schönfeld (German Lutheran) and Pastor H. L. Henriod (Swiss Reformed) as its first secretariat. That office became one of the most potent centres of influence for the development of the whole Ecumenical Movement.

The Stockholm Conference had shown that the separation of practical from doctrinal questions was not as simple a matter as some had thought. The years that followed brought growing realisation of this fact. As one reads the volumes of essays written in preparation for the Movement's second conference, held at Oxford in 1937, one notices the increasing attention paid to the theological issues underlying questions of ethics and practical policy. There is much definitely theological discussion of such subjects as the Christian doctrine of man, and eschatology.

The main theme of the Conference was defined as "Church, Community and State". One hundred and eighteen Churches from forty different countries provided four hundred and twenty-five members of whom three hundred were officially appointed delegates. These were divided into five sections for the discussion of the following subdivisions of the main theme:

(i) Church and Community.
(ii) Church and State.

(iii) Church, Community and State in relation to the Economic Order.

(iv) Church, Community and State in relation to Education.

(v) Church, Community and State in relation to the World of Nations.

The Oxford Conference had six presidents:

> The Archbishop of Canterbury (Lang).
> Archbishop Germanos.
> Archbishop Eidem of Uppsala.
> Bishop Azariah of Dornakal, S. India (Anglican).
> Dr. William Adams Brown (Presbyterian Church in the U. S. A.).
> Pastor Marc Boegner (French Reformed Churches).

The chairmen of the above mentioned five Sections of the Conference were:

> (i) Sir Walter Moberly (London)
> (ii) Professor Max Huber (Zürich)
> (iii) Mr. John R. P. Maud (Oxford)
> (iv) President Henry Sloane Coffin (New York)
> (v) President John Mackay (Princeton)

C. *The World Conference on Faith and Order.*

At the Edinburgh Missionary Conference in 1910 Bishop Charles Henry Brent of the Protestant Episcopal Church in the U. S. A.[5] became the leader of a small group who were made restive by the exclusion of all discussion of questions of faith and order. They recognised the necessity of the restriction imposed on that conference, and loyally acquiesced in it. But they saw that so long as these questions were ignored the core of the problem of our church divisions was being evaded. There at Edinburgh was conceived in their minds the idea of a

---

[5]Bishop successively of the Philippines and of Western New York.

conference called specifically for the purpose of discussing those excluded issues.

The General Convention of the Episcopal Church was due to meet in the fall of that same year. Coming home to it from Edinburgh, Bishop Brent brought forward the idea which had been germinating in his mind, and the Convention passed a resolution to promote

> "a Conference following the general method of the World Missionary Conference, to be participated in by representatives of all Christian bodies throughout the world which accept our Lord Jesus Christ as God and Saviour, for the consideration of questions pertaining to the Faith and Order of the Church of Christ."

The Committee appointed by the Convention to consider the proposal stated in its report its conviction that

> "such a Conference for the purposes of study and discussion, without power to legislate or to adopt resolutions, is the next step towards unity."

In this action of the General Convention of the American Episcopal Church we have the origin of the Faith and Order Movement. We see what from the first have been its basis, its method, and its aim. Its ultimate aim was the organic unity of all Christendom in one undivided Church; its immediate aim was to prepare the way for this by persuading the existing divided Churches to discuss with one another their differences on questions of faith and order. Its method, consequently, was to invite Churches to confer on the understanding that nothing should be done which should make it necessary for any Church to choose between loyalty to its convictions and co-operation in the framing and passing of resolutions. The invitations were to be issued on the basis of the trinitarian faith of the Nicene

Creed: to have cast the net more widely would have rendered nugatory from the start any hope of discussion leading to unity in the field of faith.

It should be added, however, that the Movement has never attempted to be the judge of whether any Church did or did not satisfy this condition. The invitation was issued on that basis, and it was left to the Churches themselves to decide whether or no they could honestly accept it.

A case in point arose in 1935. One effect of the break up of the Austro-Hungarian Empire in the 1914-1918 war had been the formation of he Czechoslovakian National Church. In reaction against the established Roman Catholicism of the old Empire, and attracted by the thought that in unitarianism they would find the most free and modern contrast with the enforced traditionalism of the past from which they had escaped, the leaders of that Church were unwilling to see it bound to any credal formula. They had only moved in this direction after the Lausanne Conference of 1927; they wanted to continue in the Movement, but honesty compelled them to ask whether they might be allowed to. When the Continuation Committee met in Denmark in August, 1935, there was a long discussion which ended with the passing of this resolution:

> "That the thanks of the Committee be sent to Dr. Hník for his letter, and that the Committee, whilst re-affirming as the basis of the Lausanne Movement the principle that invitations to take part in it should be issued to all churches which accept our Lord Jesus Christ as God and Saviour, desires also to re-affirm its conviction that the question whether or no any particular church can participate in the work of the Movement on this basis must be decided by the church itself. The Committee earnestly hopes that as the Czechoslovakian Church took part in the 1927 World Conference it will be able to continue its participation in the Movement."

I must digress for a moment to speak of an incident in the discussion at that 1935 meeting. A most impassioned speech was made by the late Dr. Zilka. He was one of the leaders of the Czech Brethren Evangelical Church, a Lutheran Church of unquestioned orthodoxy. He appealed to us to do all we could to avoid thrusting the young Czechoslovakian National Church out of the fellowship of its orthodox fellows. He urged us to remember its youth, and to treat it as an honest enquirer after the truth who would best be helped to find it by the continued companionship of churches which had found that Nicene orthodoxy was not inconsistent with honest modern thought. I remember thinking to myself, as he spoke, "Could this have happened fifty years ago? Would the leader of one church have been able to resist the temptaton to seize the opportunity of exhibiting the unorthodoxy of its rival? Can this be anything but the influence of the Holy Spirit working through this ecumenical movement?"

The following statement of the four fundamental principles of the Faith and Order Movement is taken from a statement issued by its Executive Committee in February, 1937:

"(i) Its main work is to draw churches out of isolation into *conference*, in which none is to be asked to be disloyal to or to compromise its convictions, but to seek to explain them to others while seeking to understand their points of view. Irreconcilable differences are to be recorded as honestly as agreements.

(ii) Its conferences are to be conferences of delegates officially appointed by the churches to represent them.

(iii) Invitations to take part in these conferences are to be issued to "all Christian bodies throughout the world which accept our Lord Jesus Christ as God and Saviour".

(iv) Only churches themselves are competent to take actual steps towards reunion by entering into negotiations with one another. The work of the movement is not to formulate schemes and tell the churches what they ought to do, but to act as the handmaid of the churches in the preparatory work of clearing away misunderstandings, discussing obstacles to reunion, and issuing reports which are *submitted to the churches for their approval*.⁶"

Before it adjourned the 1910 General Convention of the Episcopal Church appointed a Commission to take charge of its proposal, and issued an invitation to other churches to appoint similar commissions to co-operate with it. The 1914-1918 war delayed proceedings, but as soon as it was over

"The last adventure on a large scale was a deputation to Europe and the East, in the spring and summer of 1919. The members of this embassy were the Bishops of Chicago, Southern Ohio and Fond du Lac, with the Rev. Drs. E. L. Parsons and B. Talbot Rogers: and they were joined in Athens by their secretary Mr. Ralph W. Brown. . . . The Report of this deputation . . . is the record of a difficult, adventurous, and astonishingly successful journey. The deputation as a whole visited Athens, Smyrna, Constantinople, Sofia, Bucarest, Belgrade and Rome. At Rome the deputation divided, the Bishop of Fond du Lac and Dr. Rogers going to Alexandria, Cairo, Jerusalem and Damascus, while the others went to Paris, London, Norway, and Sweden. The results of this deputation have been manifest alike at Geneva and Lausanne, in the full and friendly co-operation which has been secured with the Orthodox Eastern Churches and with the Churches of Scandinavia. In Rome, through the great courtesy of Archbishop Cerretti, a formal invitation and statement about the Conference was presented to his Holiness the Pope through Cardinal Gasparri: and the official refusal of the invitation was balanced by the personal friendliness and benevolence of the Pope.⁷"

⁶L. Hodgson: *The Second World Conference on Faith and Order* (New York, 1938) pp. 3, 194.

⁷H. N. Bate: *Faith and Order, Lausanne 1927* (New York, 1927), pp. ix, x.

A preliminary conference was held at Geneva in 1920, attended by representatives of seventy churches from forty nations. This proved the possibility of the kind of inter-church discussion intended by Bishop Brent and his colleagues, and encouraged all concerned to go forward.

The first World Conference on Faith and Order was held at Lausanne, Switzerland, in 1927. Bishop Brent was President, assisted by the English Congregationalist, Dr. A. E. Garvie, as Deputy-Chairman. There were four Vice-Presidents: Archbishop Söderblom, Archbishop Germanos, Pastor Charles Merle d'Aubigné of the French Reformed Churches, and the German Lutheran Dr. Adolf Deissmann.

In accordance with its plans and principles the Conference issued a report which stated with equal explicitness agreements reached and continuing disagreements. This was submitted to the Churches, who were asked to take it into consideration and send in their considered judgments upon it. A Continuation Committee was appointed, with instructions to receive these communications from the Churches and plan the future of the Movement in the light of them. In 1929, when Bishop Brent had died, Dr. William Temple, then Archbishop of York, succeeded him as Chairman of the Continuation Committee.

When I became secretary to this committee in 1933 it had as its four Vice Chairmen Dr. Deissmann, Archbishop Germanos, Pastor Charles Merle d'Aubigné, and Dr. J. Ross Stevenson. The Replies of the Churches to the Lausanne Report had been collected by Dean H. N. Bate of York, and one of my first tasks was to complete his editorial work and arrange for their publication in the volume entitled *Convictions*.

The Continuation Committee had met annually from 1928 to 1931. Reflecting on the Lausanne discussions and the reception of the Report by the Churches it had decided that the subject for discussion at the next World Conference should be

"The Church in the Purpose of God". A tentative programme had been sketched out, and under the chairmanship of Bishop Headlam of Gloucester international theological commissions were studying the doctrine of Grace, and the Ministry and Sacraments. Financial stringency prevented any meetings of the Committee in 1932 and 1933. When it re-assembled in 1934 it soon became clear that the problems to be faced were more complex than had been realised. Roughly speaking, Churches on the continent of Europe held that the chief obstacles to unity lay in doctrinal disagreements on such subjects as the Word of God and *Sola Gratia*; Anglo-Saxon Churches were most concerned about questions of orders; voices from America called attention to Churches identical in both faith and order but divided by historical, cultural and psychological factors. Each group tended to demand the chief place on the programme for its own concern.

In 1935 it was decided that the Second World Conference should be held at Edinburgh in the summer of 1937, and that its programme should be built up so as to include all the concerns that had come to light the year before. These plans were carried out. The Conference met from August 3rd to 18th under the presidency of Archbishop Temple. There were present 344 delegates from 123 Churches in 44 countries. The Vice-Presidents were Dr. Garvie, Bishop Aulen (Church of Sweden), Pastor Boegner, Archbishop Germanos, and Dr. J. Ross Stevenson (Presbyterian Church in the U. S. A.). Again there was drawn up and submitted to the Churches a Report which aimed at recording continuing disagreements as clearly as agreements reached, and again there was appointed a Continuation Committee to receive the replies of the Churches and carry on the work of the Movement.

In this lecture I have tried to show how, out of the seven great Families of Churches in our divided Christendom, what we now call the Ecumenical Movement began as a number of independent Movements which may be classified as of three main types. I have given brief outlines of the history of three of these Movements during the period of their independent development. During the latter part of that period each of these Movements was becoming increasingly aware of its belonging, with the others, to what was fundamentally One Movement, and concerned with problems in their mutual relationship arising out of this growing awareness. I have so far deliberately omitted all mention of this element in the history. It will form the main theme of the first part of my next lecture.

LECTURE II: 1937—1948

(i)

I have shown how the Ecumenical Movement began with the rise of a number of independent movements. The theme of this lecture will be the steps by which the discovery of their underlying unity found expression in the formation of the World Council of Churches.

The two movements primarily concerned were the Universal Christian Council for Life and Work (known for short as the Life and Work Movement, or the Stockholm Movement) and the World Conference on Faith and Order (Faith and Order Movement, Lausanne Movement). We have seen how the former began with the intention of avoiding doctrinal questions and concentrating on practical issues, while the latter was started specifically for the purpose of doctrinal discussions. For a while this seemed to give a clear line of demarcation, on the basis of which each could independently make claims on the man power and money of the Churches. But we have also seen how experience proved the impossibility for the Life and Work Movement of divorcing practical from doctrinal issues. When I became secretary to Faith and Order in 1933 I found a situation existing in which two dangers threatened: (i) the danger of confusion on the part of Churches when approached by two bodies claiming support for ecumenical work, and (ii) the danger of friction between Movements staking out rival claims for the limited amount of men's time and money which the Churches could be expected to give.

These dangers were apparent to most of us. But the solution of the problem was not easy. In their independent careers the two Movements had developed differing characteristics which could not easily be combined in one organisation. Life and

Work was without the trinitarian basis which was fundamental to Faith and Order. While Faith and Order was forbidden to pass resolutions or do more than submit to the Churches factual statements about agreements and disagreements, Life and Work regarded it as one of its duties to issue to the world pronouncements intended to express the judgment of the Christian conscience on current issues.

Corporate bodies, as well as individuals, seem at times to be moved by a kind of instinct of self-preservation. After 1932 Faith and Order had no permanent headquarters or full-time officials. Its officers were all men occupying posts in their own Churches; its offices were the studies of its secretaries in an English canonry and an American rectory. Life and Work had its own office in Geneva, in charge of full-time secretaries. It bulked as the larger concern, and certain of the leaders in the Faith and Order Movement viewed with suspicion any *rapprochement*. They feared it would mean that Faith and Order would be swallowed up by Life and Work, that its distinctive characteristics would be lost, and that without them the service it had been able to render to the Churches could no longer be given.

It does not need much reading between the lines to see this point of view peeping out through the following resolution passed by the Faith and Order Continuation Committee in 1935 in response to an invitation received from Life and Work:

"That the thanks of the Committee be sent to Dr. Schönfeld for his invitation to co-operate in the work of the Oecumenical Seminar at Geneva; that Dr. Schönfeld be informed that the Committee deeply appreciates the value of the work which this Seminar is doing, is glad to know that Dr. William Adams Brown will be lecturing at it, and commends it to the notice of the members of the Faith and Order Movement, but considers that the Movement itself is at present too fully occupied with the work of its own programme to be able to commit itself corporately to undertaking any share in the work of this Seminar."

But discussions continued between the officers of the two Movements, and resolutions passed in the following year, 1936, by the same Faith and Order Continuation Committee mark a distinct step forward.

"29. That the Committee would welcome the constitution of a Consultative Group composed of members representing the World Conference on Faith and Order, the Universal Christian Council for Life and Work, the World Alliance for promoting International Friendship through the Churches, the International Missionary Council, and the World Student Christian Federation; requests its Chairman to take steps to arrange for the meeting of this Group; and authorises the Chairman and Secretary to arrange for the Faith and Order Movement to be represented on it by themselves or other officers of the Movement. . . .

31. That the Continuation Committee of the World Conference on Faith and Order agrees in recommending:

(i) The appointment of a Committee to review the work of oecumenical co-operation since the Stockholm and Lausanne Conferences, and to report to the Oxford and Edinburgh Conferences regarding the future of the oecumenical movement.

(ii) That the Committee be composed of 30 members, of whom it is recommended that 20 would be chosen as occupying positions of ecclesiastical responsibility in the different Churches, 5 as representing the point of view of laymen, women, and youth, and 5 from among the officers of the oecumenical movements who would bring to the deliberations of the Committee their experience of the actual working of these movements.

(iii) That the members of the Committee be nominated by the proposed Consultative Group, in consultation with the Committees of the oecumenical movements and with the Churches.

Note. The Continuation Committee of Faith and Order, in joining with the other oecumenical organisations in appointing this Committee of Thirty, would point out that the Faith and Order Continuation Committee comes to an end with the assembly of the Edinburgh Conference, and that the future of the Movement rests entirely in the hands of the officially appointed representatives of the Churches there assembled.

32. That the following resolution passed by the French *Comité des Amis du Mouvement de Lausanne* be received and transmitted to the Consultative Group for its consideration: '(This Committee) having taken into consideration the proposal made by Professors Ménégoz and de Félice, asks the Continuation Committee whether it will not be possible, on the basis of the Declaration on the Koinônia tôn Ekklesiôn which it is hoped will be approved by the World Conference in 1937, to establish a permanent oecumenical council which will represent the great Christian communities, embody the spiritual unity already arrived at, and by its existence proclaim to the world our unswerving fidelity to the living and eternal Christ.' "

So far as I remember, the words "the oecumenical movement" in this resolution 31(i) of 1936 are the first appearance of the phrase in any official Faith and Order document. It is to be noticed that they are printed without capital letters, and that in the following paragraph the words are used in the plural to denote Life and Work, Faith and Order, I.M.C., etc. Clearly we have here a transitional stage in which the phrase is finding its way into usage, but is not yet an official or technical term.

With the passing of these resolutions by the Continuation Committee in 1936 the Faith and Order Movement, for its part, took the decisive step from which all the rest followed. Life and Work was ready to go forward on the same lines, and in the fall of that year the officers of the two movements set to work to give effect to what had been agreed. With the aid of the other movements mentioned the Consultative Group was formed. Time was short, for if anything was to come of it all proposals must be ready to be submitted for consideration by the Churches' own appointed representatives when they met at Oxford and Edinburgh in July and August next.

The first thing to be done was to form the committee that was to draft these proposals. This had to be done by invitation, and great care was taken to secure that those invited should be men and women whom the churches and movements concerned would regard as having their confidence. In order to secure a fully representative gathering it was found necessary to increase the number of those invited from thirty to thirty-five, and thus came into existence what was thereafter known as the Committee of Thirty-Five.[1]

This "Committee of Thirty-Five" met for a two day session at Westfield College, Hampstead, London, with Archbishop William Temple in the chair, on July 8th, 9th and 10th, 1937. Those who were there will never forget the dramatic character of its proceedings. All through the first day spokesmen for different movements were expounding the character, principles and methods of their work, and the conditions which must be satisfied if they were to surrender their independence. The prospect seemed to grow more and more hopeless. But Archbishop Temple was one of those who had seen clearly that something must be done, and under his patient and determined leadership perseverance had its reward. Suddenly light broke on the darkness. The idea of what has come to be the World Council of Churches dawned upon our minds, the idea that Life and Work and Faith and Order might, so to speak, marry and

[1]For the list of members, see Hodgson: *The Second World Conference on Faith and Order,* p. 192.

give birth to a child who should take his parents into his home, and take care of their interests.

The implications of this idea were examined, and during the second day it was worked out in some detail into definite plans. Finally the Committee unanimously recommended that each of the two World Conferences at Oxford and Edinburgh should adopt certain proposals for the foundation of a World Council of Churches, as follows:

"1. That the Conference regards it as desirable that, with a view to facilitating the more effective action of the Christian Church in the modern world, the movements known as "Life and Work" and "Faith and Order" should be more closely related in a body representative of the Churches and caring for the interests of each movement.

2. That the Conference approves generally the following Memorandum:

The new organisation which is proposed shall have no power to legislate for the Churches or to commit them to action without their consent; but if it is to be effective, it must deserve and win the respect of the Churches in such measure that the people of greatest influence in the life of the Churches may be willing to give time and thought to its work. . . .

There are certain ecumenical movements, such as the I.M.C., the World Alliance for International Friendship through the Churches, the Y.M.C.A., the Y.W.C.A., and the Central Bureau for Inter-Church Aid, with which the new body should enter into relationship, both in order that the life in them may flow into the Churches and that those movements may derive stability and true perspective from the Churches. The actual approach to these would need to be determined with regard to the basis and function of each.

We regard as parts of the responsibility of the new body:

(i) To carry on the work of the two World Conferences.

(ii) To facilitate corporate action by the Churches.

(iii) To promote co-operation in study.

(iv) To promote the growth of ecumenical conscious-
ness in the Churches.

(v) To consider the establishment of an ecumenical
journal.

(vi) To consider the establishment of communication
with denominational federations of world-wide
scope as well as with the movements named in the
preceding paragraph.

(vii) To call World Conferences on specific subjects as
occasion requires.

3. That the Conference approves the establishment of a
World Council of Churches functioning through the following bodies:

(i) A General Assembly of representatives of the
Churches (in accordance with a plan to be determined later) of approximately two hundred members meeting every five years.

(ii) A Central Council of (approximately) sixty members which shall be a Committee of the General
Assembly when constituted, meeting annually. . . .

(iii) A Commission for the further study of Faith and
Order subjects to be appointed at Edinburgh, and
vacancies to be filled by the Central Council.

(iv) A Commission for the further study of Life and
Work subjects to be appointed by the Central
Council, with a view to facilitating common Chris-
tian action.

4. That power be given to the Central Council to call
into such relationship with itself as may seem good, other
ecumenical movements.

5. That pending the creation of any new organisation,
each movement shall carry on its own activities through
its own staff.

6. That the Conference appoint a Constituent Committee

of seven members to co-operate with a similar committee appointed at Edinburgh (or Oxford) to complete the details and bring the scheme into existence."

The history of the World Council of Churches begins with the meeting of the Committee of Thirty-Five at Westfield College, London, in the second week of July, 1937.

(ii)

When the Conference of the Life and Work Movement met at Oxford later on in July, it had no hesitation in accepting and endorsing the proposals of the Committee of Thirty-Five. The following resolutions were adopted:

"That the Conference approves the proposal of the 'Committee of Thirty-Five' in principle, and resolves to appoint a Constituent Committee of seven members to co-operate with a similar committee, if appointed by the Faith and Order Conference meeting in Edinburgh.

That the Committee be instructed to make such modifications in the plan as may seem desirable in the light of the discussions at Oxford, or in consultation with the representatives of the Faith and Order Movement, and to bring the scheme into action.

That the Business Committee be instructed to nominate the members of the Constituent Committee and report to the Conference."

At Edinburgh in August it was another story. Hesitation, and opposition to any surrender of independence, had been greater in the Faith and Order Movement. When the Edinburgh Conference met, had before it the Westfield College proposals, and was informed of their acceptance and approval by Life and Work at Oxford, the opposition came to a head. There was a battle royal. In the end the Conference gave the plan its approval, subject to certain conditions being satisfied in the constitution to be drawn up for the proposed World Council. Chief among these conditions were:

"(i) There should be in the World Council a Commission on Faith and Order to carry on the work of the Faith and Order Movement.

(ii) This Commission should have its own secretariat and adequate finance for its work.

(iii) In the first instance the Continuation Committee appointed by the Edinburgh Conference should be the World Council's Commission on Faith and Order.

(iv) All members of the Commission on Faith and Order should belong to Churches which "accept our Lord Jesus Christ as God and Saviour".

(v) In matters of common interest to all the Churches and pertaining to Faith and Order, the whole Council should proceed in accordance with that theological basis."

It was further ordered that the Continuation Committee should be charged with the duty of deciding whether the constitution drawn up for the World Council fulfilled these conditions. If it were satisfied, the marriage of Faith and Order and Life and Work was to be consummated, and the Edinburgh Continuation Committee become the World Council's Commission on Faith and Order on the first meeting of the World Council Assembly. Until that Assembly should meet the work of the Movement, in the charge of the Continuation Committee, was to be carried on independently, as before.

Seven members, each with an alternate, were appointed to the proposed Constituent Committee, and were authorised, in conjunction with those from the Oxford Conference, to work out the details of the plan for the World Council, submit the completed plan to the Continuation Committee and, if approved by that Committee, to the Churches.

Thus was formed the Committee of Fourteen, the body commissioned by the Life and Work and Faith and Order Movements to bring into existence the World Council of Churches. Its members were:

APPOINTED BY THE OXFORD CONFERENCE OF THE LIFE AND WORK MOVEMENT

Principals	*Alternates*
M. Marc Boegner	Dr. A. Koechlin
Prof. Wm. Adams Brown	Dr. S. M. Cavert
Bishop Bell of Chichester	Sir Walter Moberly
Archbishop Germanos	Bishop Irenaeus of Novi Sad
Bishop Marahrens	Archbishop Eidem
Dr. John R. Mott	Mr. Charles P. Taft
Dr. J. H. Oldham	The Rev. M. E. Aubrey

APPOINTED BY THE EDINBURGH CONFERENCE OF THE FAITH AND ORDER MOVEMENT

Principals	*Alternates*
Archbishop Temple of York	Canon L. Hodgson
Bishop Stewart of Chicago	Dr. A. R. Wentz
Dr. J. Ross Stevenson	Dr. George C. Pidgeon
Professor Nörregaard	Dean Yngve Brilioth
Professor G. Florovsky	Archimandrite Cassian
Professor S. F. H. J. Berkel-bach van der Sprenkel	
Dr. George F. Barbour	Professor Bela Vasady
	Prof. George S. Duncan

(iii)

The paramount aim of the Committee of Fourteen was that whatever was done should be what the Churches themselves should wish. Instead, therefore, of settling down straight away to draft a constitution, it invited the Churches to send representatives to discuss the form it should take. These met at Utrecht, Holland, in May, 1938, and the constitution there devised was the one sent to the Churches when, shortly afterwards, they were invited to become members of the World Council.

The passage that stands out in my memory of that meeting was the debate on the theological basis of the Council. I had gone to Utrecht as secretary to the Faith and Order Movement charged with the responsibility of making clear that that Movement could only come into the World Council if the Nicene faith in our Lord Jesus Christ as God and Saviour was made the basis of its Faith and Order work. I was quite expecting the Council to be constituted on the wider scale of the Life and Work Movement, with the narrower basis written into its constitution as a requirement for its Faith and Order activities. But speaker after speaker, representing a wide variety of Churches from America, Great Britain, Germany, Scandinavia and elsewhere, demanded the acceptance of the Nicene faith as the basis of the Council itself. I took care to point out that this was not demanded by the Movement I represented as the price of our adhesion. It became abundantly clear that the basis would be adopted, not because of any desire to conciliate the stalwarts of the Faith and Order Movement, but because it was the almost unanimous demand of all those present. One speaker voiced the mind of the meeting when he said that if it was desired to have a Council of Christian Churches, they must be Christian Churches, and Christian Churches are Churches which accept that Nicene faith.

The prevailing impression made on my mind was that that debate registered the change that had come over the theological world since I had begun my theological studies in 1913. There was no one present to voice the modernist liberalism which, I felt, would almost certainly have been a prominent, if not dominant, force in any similar gathering held a quarter of a century earlier.

The constitution drafted as a result of the meeting at Utrecht in May was brought before the Faith and Order Continuation Committee in August. Some minor adjustments were suggested to make sure that the requirements of the Edinburgh Conference were met. These were agreed to by the Committee of Fourteen. The way was clear for invitations to be issued to the Churches to join what was officially described as the "World Council of Churches in process of formation".

The Committee of Fourteen, which was officially responsible for this "formation" enlarged itself by associating together its principals and alternates, and co-opting three more members from each of the two Movements. Thus was formed the so-called "Provisional Committee".

This Provisional Committee held one meeting at St. Germain-en-Laye, near Paris, in January, 1939. It was then that Dr. W. A. Visser 't Hooft was appointed to be General Secretary of the "World Council of Churches in process of formation", with two Associate Secretaries, Dr. William Paton in London and Dr. Henry S. Leiper in New York. Plans were confidently laid for the convening of the first Assembly of the World Council in 1941. Then Faith and Order would be fully integrated into its structure and the process of formation would be completed.

But this was not to be. The outbreak of the second world war in September cut across the plans made in January. The "process of formation" was to take longer than any of us had foreseen.

It was indeed fortunate that the Provisional Committee had taken charge of proceedings and had established its secretariat with its offices in Geneva, London and New York. Not only was it able to carry on, so far as war conditions would permit, the previous activities of the Life and Work Movement, but those war conditions themselves produced needs which only something like a World Council of Churches could meet.

Thanks to the insight, the initiative, the organising ability, and the energy of Dr. Visser 't Hooft and his colleagues, the Council "in process of formation" rose to the occasion. From the vantage point of its office in neutral Switzerland, its staff could keep in touch with Church leaders on both sides of the shifting battle front. Sectional meetings of members of the Provisional Committee were held now here, now there, co-ordinated by travelling members of the neutral staff. The old work of the Study Department and the Press Service was continued; the new need of pastoral care for prisoners of war and refugees demanded the improvisation of new machinery and method, and this need was met. When fighting ceased in 1945 there were still prisoners of war; refugees became displaced persons; the reconstruction of church work in occupied countries and devastated areas began. The World Council may have been officially "in process of formation", but there was already more of substance than of shadow to it.

The postponement of the Assembly involved the postponement of the integration of the Faith and Order Movement into the World Council. During the ten years from 1938 to 1948 it had to continue its independent existence, carrying on its work as best it could. Its method was summarised in a document issued by its Executive Committee in 1946:

"(i) The World Conference discovers what measure of agreement can be reached on matters divisive of Church unity, and at what points irreconcilable disagreements call for further study. These reports are submitted to the Churches.

(ii) The Continuation Committee receives from the Churches statements of their judgments on the Reports of the World Conference, and refers outstanding points of disagreement to small international commissions of theologians for their consideration.

(iii) When, in the judgment of the Continuation Committee, the time is ripe for the calling of another World Conference, this is done, and the reports of the Commissions on the subjects entrusted to them form the basis of its discussions."

At its meetings in 1938 and 1939 the Continuation Committee, reflecting on the outcome of the Edinburgh Conference, set up three theological commissions: (i) On the Church, (ii) On Ways of Worship, (iii) On Intercommunion.

Dr. R. Newton Flew, of Cambridge, England, was appointed Chairman of the Commission on the Church, and an American Committee, with Dr. George W. Richards, of Lancaster, Pennsylvania, as Chairman, was formed to work in co-operation.

The Commission on Ways of Worship was intended to promote a growth in mutual understanding between the Churches by grasping the doctrinal issues underlying their different practices. Professor Van der Leeuw, of Groningen, Holland, was appointed Chairman of this Commission.

The war began before the Commission on Intercommunion could be fully formed. An American section, under the chairmanship of Dr. Hugh Thomson Kerr, of Pittsburgh, Pennsylvania, was able to get to work at once, but the constitution of a corresponding European section had to be postponed.

Thus, during the war years, the work of the Faith and Order Movement had to consist of collecting and preparing material for use when fully international meetings should again be possible. A Movement whose very *raison d'être* is to give all possible Churches the opportunity of conferring together, would have stultified itself if, on the conclusion of hostilities, the representatives of some had felt themselves to be presented with a *fait accompli* from others. What could be done was done. Valuable interim reports were printed by the American Committee on the Church, and by the American Section of the Commission on Intercommunion. By the fall of 1945 these and other papers were in hand, many personal contacts had been maintained, and the work was ready to go forward on the lines laid down in 1939.

(iv)

In February, 1946 was held at Geneva the second full meeting of the World Council Provisional Committee, the first that had been possible since January, 1939. Among those present were:

Dr. John R. Mott	Pastor Boegner
Dr. Douglas Horton	Dr. Kraemer
Mr. C. P. Taft	Pfarrer Traar
Dr. A. R. Wentz	Archbishop Germanos
Dr. J. W. Gallagher	Bishop Cassian
The Archbishop of Canterbury	Dr. Florovsky
The Bishop of Chichester	Professor Alivisatos
Dr. R. Newton Flew	Professor Zander
Dr. E. J. Hagan	Dr. T. Ionescu
Mrs. Bliss	Bishop Wurm
Canon L. Hodgson	Pastor Menn
Bishop Berggrav	Pastor Niemöller
Archbishop Eidem	Professor Baez-Camargo
Bishop Brilioth	Dr. P. D. Devanandan
Bishop Fuglsang-Damgaard	Dr. Chester Miao
Bishop Küry	Dr. G. K. T. Wu

The Archbishop of Canterbury and Archbishop Germanos were associated with two of the Swiss Reformed Cathedral clergy in the conduct of an evening service, for which the Cathedral was packed from door to door. No one who was present will ever forget that service, with the three moving addresses by Dr. Miao, Bishop Berggrav and Pastor Niemöller.

Many of us had travelled to Geneva with some apprehension: how should we meet, we who had so recently been enemies, who represented victors and vanquished, occupied countries and occupying powers? What I personally remember most vividly was the astounding *naturalness* of it all. We simply met as fellow servants of our one Lord, as though all other considerations were irrelevant, and it was the most natural thing in the world to meet and carry on His interrupted work no matter what had been the character of the interruption.

A very friendly letter of greeting was read from the Roman Catholic bishop whose diocese includes Geneva.

Besides the meeting of the World Council Provisional Committee there was held at that time and place a meeting of the Faith and Order Executive Committee. This surveyed the existing state of the work of the Commissions, made the adjustments, plans and appointments that were necessary to meet the needs of the post-war work, and arranged for the full Continuation Committee to meet at Clarens, Switzerland, in August, 1947. Since the death of Archbishop Temple in 1944 the Committee had been without a Chairman. At Clarens in 1947 it was decided unanimously to ask Bishop Yngve Brilioth of Växjö, Sweden, to fill that office. With his consent the appointment was announced. From that time onwards it was full steam ahead in preparation for the first Assembly of the World Council of Churches, now scheduled to meet in Amsterdam, Holland, in August, 1948.

LECTURE III: 1948—1950

(i)

IN 1948, from August 23rd to September 4th, the first Assembly of the World Council of Churches met at Amsterdam in Holland. By this time nearly one hundred and fifty Churches, from all over the world, had accepted membership in the Council "in process of formation", and were represented. There were seated on the platform and in the centre of the floor of the *Concertgebouw* 351 delegates, 238 alternates, and a number of experts who were present as consultants. Round the sides and in the galleries were a youth group of 100, some 600 visitors and about 250 press men. On August 23rd Pastor Marc Boegner formally moved the resolution constituting the Council. "In process of formation" was ended. The World Council of Churches was in being.

Future ages will, I believe, look back on the year 1948 as opening a new period in Church history. We can divide what has gone before into three. For rather more than nine hundred years, roughly half of its history up to date, the Christian Church was one. For the next six hundred years or so it was divided between East and West. Then came the break up of the Western Church and, as we saw in my first lecture, in the next four hundred years the separated Churches were mostly engaged independently in developing their own distinctive traditions. Now, on August 23rd, 1948, a large number of Churches from East and West recognised one another as brothers, pledged themselves to work together and seek the way to full union, and set up a permanent organisation to carry this on.

The Assembly elected a *praesidium* of six presidents, who took turns in presiding over its sessions. These were:

Pastor Marc Boegner, of the Reformed Church of France.

Professor T. C. Chao, of the Anglican Church in China (Chung Hua Sheng Kung Hui).

The Most Rev. Erling Eidem, Archbishop of Uppsala, Church of Sweden.

The Most Rev. Geoffrey Fisher, Archbishop of Canterbury, Church of England.

The Most Rev. Germanos, Archbishop of Thyatira, Exarch of the Patriarch of Constantinople.

Dr. John R. Mott, of the Methodist Church, U. S. A.

After some opening meetings in full session, in which the Assembly made a general survey of the past history and future prospects of the ecumenical movement, it was divided into four committees and four sections which met separately. The committees dealt with the constitution, organisation and finance of the movement, the sections with questions concerning the nature of the church, its evangelistic work, and its relation to contemporary political, social and international problems. Then in the final week the Assembly in full session received the reports of the committees and sections, debated and amended them, and so approved the form in which its own report should be issued to the world.

Two passages from this Report, where it deals with the nature of the Church, illustrate what I have said about the opening of a new period in church history:

"Although we cannot fully meet, Our Lord will not allow us to turn away from one another. We cannot ignore one another, for the very intensity of our differences testifies to a common conviction which we draw from them. The Body of Christ is a unity which makes it impossible for us either to forget each other or to be content with agreement upon isolated parts of our belief whilst we leave the other parts unreconciled."

"The World Council of Churches has come into existence because we have already recognized a responsibility to one another's churches in Our Lord Jesus Christ. There is but one Lord and one Body. Therefore we cannot rest content with our present divisions. Before God we are responsible for one another. We see already what some of our responsibilities are, and God will show us more. But we embark upon our work in the World Council of Churches in penitence for what we are, in hope for what we shall be. At this inaugural Assembly, we ask for the continual prayer of all participating churches that God may guide it in His wisdom, saving us both from false claims, and from faithless timidity."

When the reports of the Committees came before the full Assembly it was decided to make no change in the basic requirement that membership should be restricted to Churches which "accept our Lord Jesus Christ as God and Saviour".

As a permanent organisation the Assembly appointed a Central Committee of ninety members, and gave it power to appoint its own Executive. This was to meet annually, and take charge of the work of the Council until, five years later, the Churches should send freshly appointed delegates to another Assembly. A budget was adopted, based on the expectation that member Churches would contribute annually 300,000 dollars. Authority was given for the establishment of the following Departments, to work under the general direction of the Central Committee:

(a) A General Secretariat
(b) The Commission on Faith and Order
(c) A Study Department
(d) A Youth Department
(e) A Department for Inter-Church Aid and Service to Refugees
(f) The Churches' Commission on International Affairs
(g) The Ecumenical Institute
(h) A Department of Finance and Business
(i) A Department on Prisoners of War

(j) A Department of Information

(k) A Commission on the Work of Women in the Church

(l) A Secretary for Evangelism.

The Assembly decided that the Council should continue to have a *praesidium* of six. Dr. Mott was raised to the dignity of Honorary President, and Bishop G. Bromley Oxnam, of the Methodist Church, U. S. A., was elected to join the other six presidents of the Assembly and form the Council's continuing *praesidium*.

The Right Rev. G. K. A. Bell, Bishop of Chichester, England, was made Chairman of the Central Committee, with Dr. Franklin C. Fry, of the United Lutheran Church of America as Vice-Chairman.

The Rev. Dr. W. A. Visser 't Hooft, who had so ably steered the Council through the troubled years of its "process of formation", was now formally established as General Secretary. The central office of the Council is at 17 route de Malagnou, Geneva, Switzerland. As Associate Secretaries Dr. H. S. Leiper is in charge of its office at 297 Fourth Avenue, New York 10, N. Y., U. S. A., and the Rev. O. S. Tomkins of another at 39 Doughty Street, London, W. C. 1, England.

(ii)

With the meeting of the Amsterdam Assembly the Faith and Order Movement was at last integrated into the structure of the World Council of Churches. The Edinburgh Continuation Committee held a last meeting at Amsterdam on August 21st, and re-convened as the Council's Commission on Faith and Order a few miles away at Baarn on September 7th. At this meeting I gladly handed over the general secretaryship of the Commission to the Rev. Oliver S. Tomkins. The Rev. Dr. Floyd W. Tomkins, of Washington, Connecticut, was continued in office as Associate Secretary in America, and I was appointed to continue as Theological Secretary.

Reports were received from the three Theological Commissions, some of the papers contributed to them were read, and there was lively discussion. During the ensuing year these Commissions continued their work, held meetings of their own, and reported to the full Commission at Chichester, England, in July, 1949. At that meeting it was decided that the Central Committee of the World Council should be asked to summon a Third World Conference on Faith and Order for 1952, and that the invitation received from Bishop Nygren to hold it at Lund, Sweden, should be accepted. The three Theological Commissions were instructed to complete their work and produce their reports on the Church, Ways of Worship, and Intercommunion, in the course of 1950. It was further agreed that in addition there should be brought before the Lund Conference material concerning some non-theological factors which are obstacles to Church unity.

Immediately after the adjournment of the Amsterdam Assembly the World Council's Central Committee held its first meeting near by at Woudschoten. It met again at Chichester, England, in July, 1949, where the large attendance of Church leaders from all over the world showed the importance they attach to this ecumenical work. Its third meeting is to be held this summer in Canada.

I have no time to speak of other important activities now being carried on by the various Departments of the World Council, of its Press Service, its work for Inter-Church Aid, for Displaced Persons, or of the courses held at the Ecumenical Institute at Bossey, Switzerland. I must content myself with mentioning two which have been of special interest to myself.

Last summer, 1949, the Study Department held a small conference of theologians in Oxford, England. I was away from

Oxford at the time, and could not be present. Now, as a professor of theology in that university, I should like to bear testimony to the value of a pamphlet which has been issued as part of the report of that gathering, entitled *Guiding Principles for the Interpretation of the Bible*. On both sides of the Atlantic teachers of theology are puzzled to know what to do about pupils who in examinations politely reproduce what they have been taught of biblical criticism, but for their own religious purposes lapse back into a fundamentalist use of the Bible. We shall not be able to solve this puzzle until we can lay along side of fundamentalism an intelligent reading of the Bible which is equally coherent, positive and constructive. To have laid the foundations of this on an international and interdenominational basis is a piece of work well worth doing.

During a week-end in September I was present at an informal and unofficial gathering in Paris of Roman Catholic and other theologians. I do not know how far it will be possible for such conversations to be continued in the future. That depends on the interpretation that will be put on the recent Papal pronouncement on the subject.[1] All of us who were there came away with a deep sense of what we had gained, not only from the interchange of ideas with brother theologians, but also from the growth in mutual understanding between Christians of different traditions which only personal intercourse can give. The meeting, as I have said, was informal and unofficial. It was in no sense a World Council activity. But I think it is true to say that without the channels of communication established by the World Council organisation so varied a representation of different countries and churches could not have been assembled together as we were.

---

[1] *De Motione Ecumenico.* See the *Ecumenical Review*, Vol. II, No. 3, p. 296.

(iii)

I have done what I can to set before you a brief sketch of the history of the Ecumenical Movement during these last forty years, its formative period. I will now end these lectures with some reflections upon the resulting situation as it confronts us to-day.

First and foremost I want to emphasize my conviction that we are witnessing the opening of a new period in Church history. I have explained why I think this, and need not go over that ground again. But I should make it clear that to my mind what constitutes the novelty is not the particular form of organisation which has appeared in the World Council, but the new type of interest in one another which has grown up in our divided Churches. The fact that the Holy Spirit has moved the Churches to feel this interest and to seek to devise forms of organisation in which it can find expression is the underlying reality of the whole Ecumenical Movement.

As for the World Council itself, I can explain it best to my fellow Anglicans when I say that it is intended to do for Christendom as a whole what the Lambeth Conferences do for our Anglican Communion. We Anglicans know that a Lambeth Conference of Bishops has no constitutional place in our polity. It has neither legislative, nor judicial, nor executive power. When we agree with its resolutions we say, "Nothing could have greater weight of authority than the considered judgment of our Fathers in God, given after these weeks of solemn conference together." When we disagree, we say, "Of course this has no authority: it simply represents the opinions of these particular bishops who happened to come together in this particular year. Ten years hence we may find their successors saying something quite different." Yet no one of us would say that, because the Lambeth Conferences have no constitutional authority, they are a waste of time. We know how

BIBLIOTHECA
Ottaviensis

greatly the whole Anglican Communion is helped and strength-
ened through these periodical opportunities of consultation between our Bishops, and we are grateful for the guidance we
receive in their Reports. If the World Council can do as
much for the wider circle of Churches, it will be to the benefit
of all.

Secondly, I would say that the great need of the Ecumenical
Movement at the moment is that it should be more fully shared
in by the general membership of our various Churches. I have
spoken of the growth in mutual understanding that can only
come by personal intercourse, and in saying that I was speaking
out of my own experience. I look back on myself as I was before
I came into the Faith and Order Movement in 1933, and I
see how abysmally ignorant I was of Christian traditions other
than Anglican when I only knew of them by book learning. It
is only through personal intercourse that one begins to learn
what other ways of holding and practising the Christian faith
look like and feel like from within. It is only by learning that
that one can begin to understand them. And it is only by growth
in such understanding that we can begin to find the way to that
Church unity for which we hope and pray.

But to how small a proportion of church members has so
far been given the opportunity and privilege of this ecumenical
education! Here let me quote from a sermon which I preached
before the University of Oxford in February, 1945:

"Few, if any, in May of last year, would have dared to
predict the stupendous change that came over the face of
the war in Western Europe between then and September.
Except for the armies slowly and painfully battling their
way up through Italy, the allies had no foothold on the
continent. For nearly four years the Germans, apparently
secure behind their defences, had maintained their grip
upon the occupied lands. Then in those four months
came the landing on the coast of Normandy, the turning

of the enemy's flank, the incredibly rapid sweep through Northern France, the junction with the force that landed in the South, the liberation of the whole of France and Belgium and the advance through Southern Holland across the Waal right up to the lower Rhine. It was no wonder that optimistic spirits, seeing how quickly how much had been accomplished, began to think that final victory was near at hand and felt deep disappointment when our armies had to settle down to a kind of siege warfare before the prepared defences of the so-called Siegfried line.

But those with inside knowledge of the situation, who viewed it as experts in military science, told us that the optimism had been as premature as the depression was unjustified. The difficulties of the autumn were the natural and inevitable result of the speed with which the successes of the summer had been achieved. The advance had been so rapid that the spear-head of attack had outstripped the possibiliy of keeping it supplied along so lengthy a line of communication with all that was needed for the invasion of Germany itself. There must of necessity be a pause to allow of adequate reinforcements being brought up to the line of battle, reinforcements not only of men, but of guns and tanks and all the multifarious equipment of modern warfare.

I have reminded you of this recent history as a parable to illustrate the progress of the movement for the reunion of divided Christendom. There are indeed some remarkable correspondences. For four years the Germans seemed to be permanently settled in occupation of Europe, disturbed only by such passing incidents as the attacks on Dieppe and S. Nazaire. For four centuries, apart from some tentative and abortive efforts at reconciliation between particular bodies, the divided churches of Christendom pursued their several ways with little interest in one another beyond the interest of pointing out their errors. In four months the rapid advance of the liberating armies so changed the face of Europe that hopes were raised of speedy victory and peace. In forty years such progress was made in the drawing together of divided churches that enthusiastic souls began to think that remaining differences could be ignored. But in both cases the success had been achieved by those in the van getting far ahead of their main body of support, and the leaders knew that tasks lay ahead of such difficulty that there must be a pause before it would be possible to go forward again."

What is needed is that the same kind of personal intercourse and mutual understanding which have been growing up among leaders drawn from the various churches in these national and international gatherings should be reproduced at all levels of church life. Bishops, other clergy, and laity need to get to know one another in this way at diocesan, district, and parochial levels. Here let me suggest a word of advice. I do not think that progress is best made by the formation of groups whose aim is directly the exposition to one another by their members of their different types of churchmanship. The desired growth in understanding comes much better when a group drawn from different denominations engages in the study of some subject of common interest, their minds rubbing up against each other as together they go out to explore it. It may be some theological subject, such as the Atonement, or Christology; it may be some topic of practical Christianity, such as the Christian attitude to alcohol or gambling. Perhaps, in view of the present disturbance in church circles caused by the rival claims of biblical criticism and fundamentalism—a disturbance which cuts across all denominational boundaries—an interdenominational group study of the pamphlet to which I have just referred (*Guiding Principles for the Interpretation of the Bible*) would be a most profitable activity.

Thirdly, there are one or two points on which those of us who are responsible for the work of the Ecumenical Movement need to have our eyes open to possible dangers. We must never allow ourselves to forget that the real work of Christ's Church is being done in the every-day life of parishes and congregations, that the ministering of the Word and Sacraments to Christ's flock is of more imporance than the discussion of problems, passing of resolutions, or issuing of messages by committees, commissions or assemblies. Connected with this is the need to beware of building up a *corpus* of whole-time professional ecumenists. I think myself that the World Council of Churches should have on its staff almost nothing in the way of permanently employed, whole-time officials. I say *almost* nothing, because experience may show that it is necessary to have one or two of these. But I am convinced that in general the staffs of the World Council in its offices at Geneva, New York, London or elsewhere should be composed of men and women temporarily lent by their Churches for periods of not more than five years apiece. I do not think it should be necessary for the World Council to have any pension scheme for its officers. The various Churches from which its officers will be drawn mostly have their own pension schemes. I think the Department of Business and Finance should enter into negotiations with the various Churches so that, by a series of agreements between them and the World Council, their members can keep alive during World Council service their pension rights and expectations in their own Churches.

Lastly, if we are at the beginning of a new period in Church history, it is only the beginning. We must not be surprised if, in the organisations already formed, there are a number of loose ends and untidy fragments. I have perhaps spoken rather too much as though the whole Ecumenical Movement were now concentrated in the World Council of Churches. This is by no means the case. The World Council stands in the centre and increasingly tends to become the main organ of inter-church co-operation, so that increasingly other ecumenical bodies are likely in one way or another to become related to it. Meanwhile, many of those mentioned in my first lecture continue on their way. Already there is growing up a very close relationship between the World Council of Churches and the International Missionary Council.

In the organisation of the World Council itself there are problems which will have to be faced in the coming years. It is a Council of *Churches*: its members are Churches in different lands and their representation by delegates to assemblies has to be adjusted so as to secure fair and adequate representation both of countries and of ecclesiastical traditions. But among themselves Churches are already internationally organised: there are, for example, World Lutheranism, the Presbyterian Alliance, the Baptist Union, and the Anglican Communion. The question has been raised whether representation should not be in terms of world-wide denominational organisations, instead of by the Churches in different geographical areas. Again, our historical survey has shown how the study work of the World Council has come to be divided between the Study Department and the Commission on Faith and Order. I cannot believe that this somewhat clumsy arrangement will endure for ever, and the situation may have to be reviewed when the Faith and Order Conference meets at Lund in 1952.

It is right that these lectures should end on the note of open questions. I have tried to give the facts of the past and present, for it is important that we should base our thoughts of the future on an understanding of things as they are. But it is to the future that we must look, and if, as the saying goes, the gates of the future are open, our eyes too must be open both to its opportunities and to its problems.

385

931312